D0753281

DISCOVER
THE OCEANS

Indian Ocean

by Emily Rose Oachs

BLASTOFF!
3
READERS

BELLWETHER MEDIA • MINNEAPOLIS, MN

Note to Librarians, Teachers, and Parents:

Blastoff! Readers are carefully developed by literacy experts and combine standards-based content with developmentally appropriate text.

Level 1 provides the most support through repetition of high-frequency words, light text, predictable sentence patterns, and strong visual support.

Level 2 offers early readers a bit more challenge through varied simple sentences, increased text load, and less repetition of high-frequency words.

Level 3 advances early-fluent readers toward fluency through increased text and concept load, less reliance on visuals, longer sentences, and more literary language.

Level 4 builds reading stamina by providing more text per page, increased use of punctuation, greater variation in sentence patterns, and increasingly challenging vocabulary.

Level 5 encourages children to move from "learning to read" to "reading to learn" by providing even more text, varied writing styles, and less familiar topics.

Whichever book is right for your reader, Blastoff! Readers are the perfect books to build confidence and encourage a love of reading that will last a lifetime!

This edition first published in 2016 by Bellwether Media, Inc.

No part of this publication may be reproduced in whole or in part without written permission of the publisher. For information regarding permission, write to Bellwether Media, Inc., Attention: Permissions Department, 5357 Penn Avenue South, Minneapolis, MN 55419.

Library of Congress Cataloging-in-Publication Data

Oachs, Emily Rose.
  Indian Ocean / by Emily Rose Oachs.
     pages cm. – (Blastoff! Readers: Discover the Oceans)
  Summary: "Simple text and full-color photography introduce beginning readers to the Indian Ocean. Developed by literacy experts for students in kindergarten through third grade"–Provided by publisher.
  Audience: Ages 5-8.
  Audience: K to grade 3.
  Includes bibliographical references and index.
  ISBN 978-1-62617-332-3 (hardcover : alk. paper)
  1. Indian Ocean–Juvenile literature. I. Title.
  GC721.O33 2016
  910.9165–dc23
                        2015030734

Printed in the United States of America, North Mankato, MN.

Table of Contents

Trade Routes

Thousands of years ago, Asian, African, and Arabian sailors crossed the Indian Ocean. They traded their goods in distant lands.

DID YOU KNOW?

○ The Indian Ocean of today formed more than 35 million years ago!

○ Some people believe that Egyptians first explored the Indian Ocean around 2300 BCE.

Suez Canal

○ The Suez Canal was built through Egypt in 1869. The waterway allows travel between Europe and Asia.

○ The Indian Ocean is almost six times larger than the United States!

Today, many companies have key **trade routes** in the Indian Ocean. Ships often carry oil to countries across the globe.

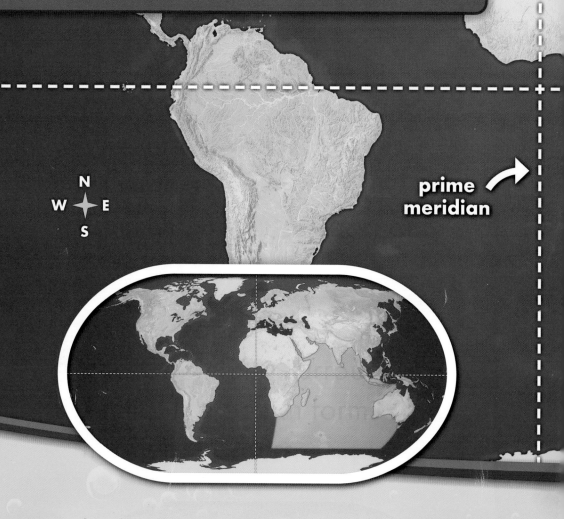

N
W · E
S

prime meridian

The Indian Ocean is in the Northern, Southern, and Eastern **hemispheres**. The **equator** crosses through it.

In the west, the Red Sea and
Africa touch the Indian Ocean.
Asia sits to its north and east.
Australia is also east.

The Climate and Features

Monsoons blow across the Indian Ocean. These winds change direction each season. In summer, they blow rain into India. In winter, they carry rain to Southeast Asia and Australia.

Cyclones also appear over the ocean's warm waters. They are strong, spinning storms!

cyclone

Underwater mountain chains run across the ocean. They rise up from the ocean floor.

Coral islands dot the Indian Ocean. They form from underwater **coral reefs**. Over time, reefs build up and islands are created.

coral reef

coral
islands

oil rig

Large stores of oil lie under
the ocean floor. Almost half
of the world's oil is taken from
the Indian Ocean!

Most of this oil comes from the Persian Gulf. Oil is also found near India, Southeast Asia, and Australia.

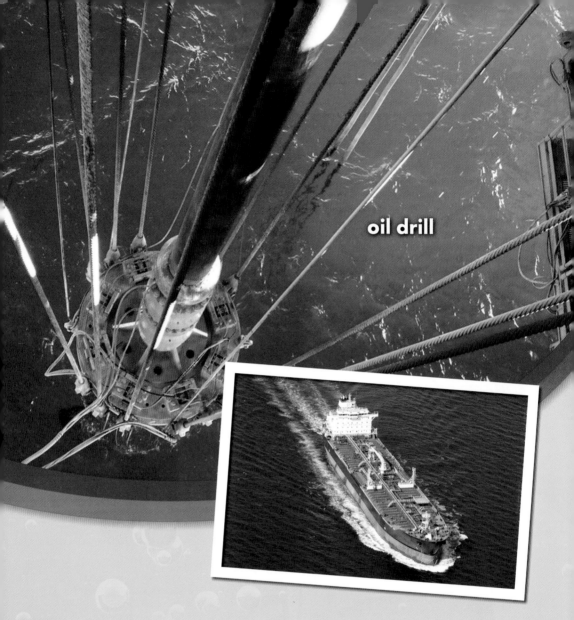

oil drill

People drill into the ocean floor to dig up the oil. Then they transfer the oil to ships. The ships carry the oil around the world.

Sometimes, the ships leak oil. This is not good for ocean life.

The Plants and Animals

Tiny plants called **phytoplankton** float on the Indian Ocean's surface. Seaweeds grow in shallow waters. Leafy sea dragons and blue-ringed octopuses live in underwater meadows of seagrass.

In **tropical** areas, coral reefs form. They house sea urchins, sponges, and lionfish.

leafy
sea dragon

blue-ringed
octopus

lionfish

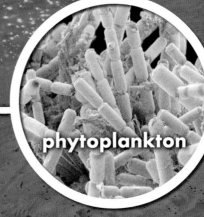
phytoplankton

Flying fish jump over the water. Sailfish and hammerhead sharks swim below the Indian Ocean's surface.

flying fish

sailfish

hammerhead shark

hawksbill
sea turtle

dugong

Dugongs and hawksbill sea turtles are **endangered** animals. The Indian Ocean needs **protection** to keep its plants and animals healthy!

Fast Facts About the Indian Ocean

Size: 26.5 million square miles (68.6 million square kilometers); 3rd largest ocean

Average Depth: 12,990 feet (3,960 meters)

Greatest Depth: 24,442 feet (7,450 meters)

Major Bodies of Water: Andaman Sea, Bay of Bengal, Arabian Sea, Persian Gulf, Red Sea

Continents Touched: Africa, Asia, Australia

Total Coastline: 41,337 miles (66,526 kilometers)

Top Natural Resources: oil, natural gas, iron, coal, shrimp

Famous Shipwrecks:
- *Godavaya* (about 100 CE)
- *Batavia* (1629)
- *Salem Express* (1991)

Salem Express

Asia

Persian
Gulf

Red
Sea

Arabian
Sea

Bay of
Bengal

Andaman
Sea

Africa

Australia

Indian
Ocean

N
W · E
S

Glossary

coral islands—islands formed from coral reefs

coral reefs—structures made of coral that usually grow in shallow seawater

cyclones—spinning storms that form over water and bring strong winds and rain; cyclones move toward shore.

endangered—at risk of no longer living

equator—an imaginary line around the center of Earth; the equator divides the planet into a northern half and a southern half.

hemispheres—halves of the globe; the equator and prime meridian divide Earth into different hemispheres.

monsoons—winds that shift direction each season; monsoons bring heavy rain.

phytoplankton—tiny ocean plants that drift

protection—an act that keeps something from harm

trade routes—paths for moving goods and resources between countries

tropical—part of the tropics; the tropics is a hot, rainy region near the equator.

To Learn More

AT THE LIBRARY

Barnes, Nico. *Hammerhead Sharks.* Minneapolis, Minn.: Abdo Kids, 2015.

Jakubiak, David J. *What Can We Do About Oil Spills and Ocean Pollution?* New York, N.Y.: PowerKids Press, 2012.

Spilsbury, Louise and Richard. *Indian Ocean.* Chicago, Ill.: Capstone Heinemann Library, 2015.

ON THE WEB
Learning more about the Indian Ocean is as easy as 1, 2, 3.

1. Go to www.factsurfer.com.

2. Enter "Indian Ocean" into the search box.

3. Click the "Surf" button and you will see a list of related web sites.

With factsurfer.com, finding more information is just a click away.

Index

The images in this book are reproduced through the courtesy of: bluehand, front cover (left); OceanImpressions, front cover (right); janemill, p. 4; Igor Grochev, p. 5; Federica Grassi/ Getty Images, p. 8; pio3, p. 9; Andrea Izzotti, p. 10 (left); R. McIntyre, pp. 10-11; nattapon1975, p. 12; Rob Ellis, p. 14 (top); Igor Karasi, p. 14 (bottom); Fluke Samed, p. 15; AtanasBozhikovNasko, pp. 16-17; Kjersti Joergensen, p. 17 (top left); Yusran Abdul Rahman, p. 17 (top middle); John_Walker, p. 17 (top right); Micro Discovery/ Corbis, p. 17 (bottom); Anthony Pierce/ Alamy, p. 18 (top left); ByronD, p. 18 (bottom left); cdascher, p. 18 (middle); richcarey, pp. 18-19; RomanMr, p. 19 (bottom); Paul Vinten, p. 20.